What Does Love Mean?

I0154407

CHARLES PHILLIPS

TEACH Services, Inc.
P U B L I S H I N G
www.TEACHServices.com • (800) 367-1844

Copyright © 2022 Charles Phillips
Copyright © 2022 TEACH Services, Inc.
ISBN-13: 978-1-4796-1460-8 (Paperback)
ISBN-13: 978-1-4796-1461-5 (ePub)
ISBN-13: 978-1-4796-1462-2 (Mass Market)

TEACH Services, Inc.
P U B L I S H I N G
www.TEACHServices.com ● (800) 367-1844

TABLE OF CONTENTS

DO YOU UNDERSTAND AND KNOW WHAT IS MEANT BY THE WORD "LOVE"?

How do you know if you have "love" in your heart? Have you seen the effects of love in others and yourself? How do you understand "love"? If you have ever had cats or dogs, then you may have felt loved by them and even loved them yourself. "God is love" (1 John 4:7–8).

Webster's says love is "a strong affection for, or attachment or devotion to a person or persons." It's God's benevolent concern for mankind, man's devout attachment to God—LOVE.

The world, as a whole, does not understand "love." If the world understood love, we would not hear and see all the hate we do today, all the killing that takes place around the world. Families would not be divided, and divorce would be unheard of.

Let us search the Scriptures, the Holy Bible, and read what and how we can understand what love is and how we can love as God would have us to love!

1 John 4:8: "He who does not love does not know God, for God is love."

Look at the word "love." What is love? How do we understand and describe love to one another today? Does Scripture help us to understand what love means to the Christian? What do the Old Testament and the New Testament say about love?

Exodus 20:6: "showing mercy to thousands, to those who love Me and keep My commandments."

Leviticus 19:18: "You shall not take vengeance, nor bear any grudge against the children of your people, but you shall love your neighbor as yourself: I *am* the LORD." The Lord wants all to understand what love is, what it means to love. Our Lord tells how He shows His love to us. Deuteronomy 5:10: "showing mercy to thousands, to those who love Me and keep My commandments."

Deuteronomy 6:5: "You shall love the LORD your God with all your heart, with all your soul, and with all your strength."

Nehemiah 1:5: "O great and awesome God, *You* who keep *Your* covenant and mercy with those who love You and observe Your commandments."

Psalm 31:23: "Oh, love the LORD, all you His saints! *For* the LORD preserves the faithful."

Psalm 91:14: "Because he has set his love upon Me, therefore I will deliver him."

Psalm 103:17: "[T]he mercy of the LORD *is* from everlasting … on those who fear Him."

Psalm 119:97: "Oh, how I love Your law! It *is* my meditation all the day."

Psalm 145:20: "The LORD preserves all who love Him."

Proverbs 8:17: "I love those who love me, and those who seek me diligently will find me."

Proverbs 10:12: "Hatred stirs up strife, but love covers all sins."

Song of Solomon 2:4: "[H]is banner over me *was* love."

Song of Solomon 8:6: "For love *is as* strong as death."

Jeremiah 31:3: "Yes, I have loved you with an everlasting love; therefore with loving kindness I have drawn you."

Micah 6:8: "He has shown you, O man, what *is* good; and what does the LORD require of you but to do justly, to love mercy, and to walk humbly with your God?"

And the New Testament says the following:

Matthew 5:44: "[L]ove your enemies, bless those who curse you, do good to those who hate you, and pray for those who spitefully use you and persecute you."

Luke 7:42: "And when they had nothing with which to repay, he freely forgave them both. Tell Me, therefore,which of them will love him more?"

John 3:16: "For God so loved the world that He gave His only begotten Son, that whoever believes in Him should not perish but have everlasting life."

John 5:42: "But I know you, that you do not have the love of God in you."

John 13:35: "By this all will know that you are My disciples, if you have love for one another."

John 14:15: "If you love Me, keep My commandments." Verse 21: "He who has My commandments and keeps them, it is he who loves Me. And he who loves Me will be loved by My Father, and I will love him and manifest Myself to him." Verse 24: "He who does not love Me does not keep My words; and the word which you hear is not Mine but the Father's who sent Me."

John 15:9: "As the Father has loved Me, I also have loved you; abide in My love."

John 15:12: "This is My commandment, that you love one another as I have loved you."

Romans 5:5: "[T]he love of God has been poured out in our hearts by the Holy Spirit who was given to us."

Romans 5:8: "But God demonstrates His own love toward us, in that while we were still sinners, Christ died for us."

Romans 13:8: "Owe no one anything except to love one another, for he who loves another has fulfilled the law." Verse 10: "Love does no harm to a neighbor, therefore love *is* the fulfillment of the law."

1 Corinthians 2:9: "Eye has not seen, nor ear heard, nor have entered into the heart of man the things which God has prepared for those who love Him."

1 Corinthians 13:4: "Love suffers long *and* is kind; love does not envy; love does not parade itself, is not puffed up." Verse 8: "Love never fails." Verse 13: "And now abide faith, hope, love, these three; but the greatest of these *is* love."

2 Corinthians 5:14: "[F]or the love of Christ compels us, because we judge thus: that if One died for all, then all died."

Galatians 5:22: "But the fruit of the Spirit is love, joy, peace, longsuffering, kindness, goodness, faithfulness."

Ephesians 4:15: "[Speak] the truth in love."

Ephesians 5:25: "Husbands, love your wives, just as Christ also loved the church and gave Himself for her."

1 Timothy 1:5: "Now the purpose of the commandment is love from a pure heart, *from* a good conscience, and *from* sincere faith."

1 Timothy 6:10: "For the love of money is a root of all *kinds of* evil."

Hebrews 13:1: "Let brotherly love continue."

James 1:12: "Blessed *is* the man who endures temptation; for when he has been approved, he will receive the crown of life which the Lord has promised to those who love Him."

James 2:5: "Listen, my beloved brethren: Has not God chosen the poor of this world *to be* rich in faith and heirs of the kingdom which He promised to those who love Him?"

1 Peter 1:8: "[W]hom having not seen you love."

1 Peter 4:8: "And above all things have fervent love for one another, for 'love will cover a multitude of sins.'"

2 Peter 1:5–7: "[A]dd to your faith virtue, to virtue knowledge, to knowledge self-control, to self-control perseverance, to perseverance godliness, to godliness brotherly kindness, and to brotherly kindness love."

1 John 2:15: "Do not love the world or the things in the world. If anyone loves the world, the love of the Father is not in him."

1 John 3:16: "By this we know love, because He laid down His life for us. And we also ought to lay down *our* lives for the brethren." Verse 18: "My little children, let us not love in word or in tongue, but in deed and in truth."

1 John 4:7: "Beloved, let us love one another, for love is of God; and everyone who loves is born of God and knows God." Verse 8: "He who does not love does not know God, for God is love." Verse 18: "There is no fear in love; but perfect love cast out fear, because fear involves torment. But he who fears has not been made perfect in love." Verse 20: "If someone says, "I love God," and hates his brother, he is a liar; for he who does not love his brother whom he has seen, how can he love God whom he has not seen?" Verse 21: "And this commandment we have from Him: that he who loves God *must* love his brother also."

1 John 5:2: "By this we know that we love the children of God, when we love God and keep His commandments."

1 John 5:3: "For this is the love of God, that we keep His commandments. And His commandments are not burdensome."

2 John 6: "This is love, that we walk according to His commandments, This is the commandment, that as you have heard from the beginning, you should walk in it."

Revelation 2:4: "Nevertheless I have *this* against you, that you have left your first love."

Revelation 3:19: "As many as I love, I rebuke and chasten. Therefore be zealous and repent."

The Bible isn't a rule book; it's a love letter. It's the story of God's heart of love for His people. When we read what Jesus has done for every person that has been born on this earth, we will understand the love Jesus Christ has for every person. There is no force in living for our Lord. Everything on this earth has love in them from God. The

choice is for everyone. Everyone must decide what they will do with the love from God in their heart.

Think about our first parents: Adam and Eve. They made a choice, and we are reaping the results today. Their children, Cain and Abel, made a choice in the sacrifice which they had been told how and what to offer by their Creator. People today have to make a choice as Abel and Cain did, only the sacrifice of a lamb is no longer required because Jesus Christ is the Lamb of God and He came and was sacrificed for the sins of all mankind.

The class of worshipers today who follow the example of Cain include by far the greater portion of the world, for nearly every false religion has been based on the same principle as Cain had: that man can depend upon his own efforts for salvation. This choice man has made shows what man will become apart from following God's plan. From Adam and Eve, every person ever born has faced the same choice: Will they choose to follow God's plan for redemption to be saved or their own way? From the very beginning of the creation of man, God declares He is the "rewarder of those who diligently seek Him" (Heb. 11:6). Enoch's life and history prove there is a reward for those who love the Lord (see Gen. 5:21–24) and that the wicked have a final reward, "eternal death."

We are saved by the grace of God, and that grace is twofold. It is forgiveness—we are born with a tendency to sin, and grace offers pardon for the sins we commit (what we do). Grace is also power to keep us from sinning.

God has always loved His creation of mankind and will always do all He can to save man, but God and His love does not use force!

The longest lifespan recorded is that of a man, Methusaleh, the son of Enoch. Methuselah lived 969 years (Gen. 5:27). Methusaleh's son Lamech became the father of Noah who preached for 120 years while building the ark. But even Noah and his family carried the virus of sin. Why? Romans 3:23: "[F]or all have sinned." From Adam and Eve, all have sinned. We have a promise in Romans 5:19: "[B]y one Man's obedience many will be made righteous." We read the history of how God worked with different people in Scripture and groups of people—Israel—to help all to know that our Creator God, that loves each enough to come to this world of sin and rebellion, died for each one's sins that we can have eternal life.

Every choice that mankind has made from Eden, you and I must make today. Will we place ourselves firmly on the side of complete loyalty to our Creator God? Or will we do as the majority have done from Creation (follow the dictates of their own life)? There are only two sides when it comes to God: those who are faithful and loyal to Him and those who choose to go their own way.

ARE YOU LOOKING FOR A SAVIOR WHO LOVES WITHOUT MEASURE?

Imagine going away for a while and returning home to find that your family doesn't recognize you—to them you are a total stranger. Or imagine going to a family reunion, only to find that no one there has the faintest idea who you are. I hope nothing like that will ever happen to you. But it did happen to Jesus. John 1:10–11: "He was in the world, and the world was made through Him, and the world did not know Him. He came to His own, and His own did not receive Him." Even in His own land and among his own people, He was not accepted. Jesus came to provide salvation not just for "His own" but for the world. It was bad enough that the world did not recognize Him, but, unbelievably, even His own rejected Him.

God doesn't choose some to be saved and some to be lost. Each person—using the power of free choice that God gave at Creation—must make the choice. To every man and woman, each ultimately decides his or her own destiny. Every person has to make their own choice. 1 Corinthians 2:9: "But, as it is written: 'Eye has not seen, nor ear heard, nor have entered into the heart of man the things which God has prepared for those who love Him.'" Hebrews 7:25: "Therefore He is also able to save to the uttermost those who come to God through Him, since He always lives to make intercession for them." Exodus 20:6: "[S]howing mercy to thousands, to those who love Me." Deuteronomy 6:5: "You shall love the LORD your God with all your heart, with all your soul, and with all your strength." And what does God promise in return? Deuteronomy 7:13: "And He will love you and bless you and multiply you." See Deuteronomy 10:12–13 to study more about this topic.

What does the New Testament say? Matthew 5:44: "[L]ove your enemies, bless those who curse you, do good to those who hate you, and pray for those who spitefully use you and persecute you." "Why?" you ask? Verse 45: "[T]hat you may be sons of your Father in heaven; for He makes His sun rise on the evil and on the good, and sends rain on the just and on the unjust." Verse 46: "For if you love those who love you, what reward have you?" Matthew 6:24: "No one can serve two masters; for either he will hate the one and love the other, or else he will be loyal to the one and despise the other. You cannot serve God and mammon." We see this today in America. Matthew 24:12: "[B]ecause lawlessness will abound, the love of many will grow cold." Mark 12:30–31: "'[Y]ou shall love the LORD your God with all your heart, with all your soul, with all your mind, and with all your strength.' This *is* the first commandment. And the second, like *it*, *is* this: 'You shall love your neighbor as yourself.' There is no other commandment greater than these." Luke 6:32: "[I]f you love those who love you, what credit is that to you? For even sinners love those who love them." Luke 16:13: "No servant can serve two masters; for either he will hate the one and love the other, or else he will be loyal to the one and despise the other. You cannot serve God and mammon."

Jesus told the people that if God were their Father, they would love Him. John 14:24: "He who does not love Me does not keep My words; and the word which you hear is not Mine but the Father's who sent Me." John 15:10: "If you keep My commandments, you will abide in My love." Verse 13: "Greater love has no one than this, than to lay down one's life for his friends." Romans 5:8: "But God demonstrates His own love toward us, in that while we were still sinners, Christ died for us." Romans 13:8: "Owe no one anything except to love one another, for he who loves another has fulfilled the law." Verse 10: "Love does no harm to a neighbor; therefore love *is* the fulfillment of the law." 1 Corinthians 2:9: "Eye has not seen, nor ear heard, nor have entered into the heart of man the things which God has prepared for those who love Him." Galatians 5:22–23: "[T]he fruit of the Spirit is love, joy, peace, longsuffering, kindness, goodness, faithfulness, gentleness, self-control. Against such there is no law." 2 Thessalonians 2:10: "[A]ll unrighteous deception among those who perish, because they did not receive the love of the truth, that they might be saved." 2 Timothy 1:7: "For God has not given us a spirit of fear, but of power and of love and of a sound mind." Titus 3:5: "[N]ot by works of righteousness which we have done, but according to His mercy He saved us." Hebrews 6:10: "For God *is* not unjust to forget your work and labor of love which you have shown toward His name." James 1:12: "Blessed *is* the man who endures temptation; for when he has been approved, he will receive the crown of life which the Lord has promised to those who love Him." 1 John 2:15: "Do not love the world or the things in the world. If anyone loves the world, the love of the Father is not in him." 1 John 3:16: "By this we know love, because He laid down His life for us. And we also ought to lay down *our* lives for the brethren." Verses 17–18: "[W]hoever has this world's goods, and sees his brother in need, and shuts up his heart from him, how does the love of God abide in him? My little children, let us not love in word or in tongue, but in deed and in truth." 1 John 4:7: "Beloved, let us love one another, for love is of God; and everyone who loves is born of God and knows God." Verse 8: "He who does not love does not know God, for God is love." Verse 9: "In this the love of God was manifested toward us, that God has sent His only begotten Son into the world, that we might live through Him." Verse 10: "In this is love, not that we loved God, but that He loved us and sent His Son *to be* the propitiation for our sins." Verse 12: "No one has seen God at any time. If we love one another, God abides in us, and His love has been perfected in us." Verse 19: "We love Him because He first loved us." Verse 20: "If someone says, "I love God," and hates his brother, he is a liar; for he who does not love his brother whom he has seen, how can he love God whom he has not seen?" Verse 21: "And this commandment we have from Him: that he who loves God *must* love his brother also." 1 John 5:2–3: "By this we know that we love the children of God, when we love God and keep His commandments. For this is the love of God, that we keep His commandments. And His commandments are not burdensome." 2 John 6: "This is love, that we walk according to His commandments. This is the commandment, that as you have heard from the beginning, you should walk in it." Jude 21: "[K]eep yourselves in the love of God, looking for the mercy of our Lord Jesus Christ unto eternal life." Revelation 3:19: "As many as I love, I rebuke and chasten. Therefore be zealous and repent."

James 3:1 is a warning to people who want to be teachers of God's Word: "My brethren, let not many of you become teachers, knowing that we shall receive a stricter judgment."

HOW MANY WILL BE SAVED?

The end of the great controversy between good and evil—between Christ and Satan—isn't finished yet. In the final, dramatic showdown before Jesus returns, a vast multitude will join Christ's faithful followers. Some who have tried to avoid making a choice will make one. Revelation 7:9–10: "[A] great multitude which no one could number, of all nations, tribes, peoples, and tongues, standing before the throne and before the Lamb, clothed with white robes, with palm branches in their hands, and crying out with a loud voice, saying, 'Salvation *belongs* to our God who sits on the throne and to the Lamb!'" We need not be concerned that the loyal followers of Jesus are—and have ever been—few in number compared to those who don't know about love.

Those that have chosen not to be of those who are saved, had eyes with which to read but could not see. They had ears with which they heard the prophets, but they could not and would not hear.

What about today? Are Christians ready for Jesus to come? When Jesus came the first time as a baby, how many were looking for Him? Were the leaders of the church proclaiming Christ's coming? What about today? Do we hear in our church that Christ is coming soon? It was the humble shepherds in a field that an angel appeared to and announced Christ's birth. What about today? Are you looking for our Lord to come and redeem those who love and honor what Jesus has said in His Book?

Not everyone in the crowd, as Jesus was on the cross, called for His death. Simon the Cyrene carried the cross for Jesus (Matt. 27:32), and his steps took him to the side of right and truth and salvation. A Roman centurion chose the side of Jesus at the cross, saying, "Truly this Man was the Son of God!" (Mark 15:39). Also at the cross, being crucified beside our Lord, a thief made the same decision—as did many in the clamoring crowd at the foot of the cross (Luke 23:40–42).

The history of the church proves that, at its most corrupt time, there have always been the faithful few who have followed Jesus with a faith that cannot be shaken. As you read these words, the entire world population of 7.8 billion and counting are lining up on one side of the great controversy or

> **The end of the great controversy between good and evil— between Christ and Satan—isn't finished yet**

the other. A tragic majority are choosing the wrong side. But God has His faithful, even at this time and moment. They have a heart of love to obey Him; they will stand for His truth and defend His character to their last breath.

We read in Isaiah 1:18: "'Come now, and let us reason together,' says the LORD, 'Though your sins are like scarlet, they shall be as white as snow; though they are red like crimson, they shall be as wool.'" Verse 19: "If you are willing and obedient, you shall eat the good of the land." God has promised more than people can imagine if we only love and honor our Creator.

To honor our Lord is to love God and our fellow man. The purpose of the law of God—His commandments—in this sinful world isn't to save but to point out sin. Sin is primarily a rejection of God, a turning away from Him. How many of us has sinned? All of us have sinned; therefore, redemption cannot be based on a lack of sin; it must be based on forgiveness (Jer. 31:34). The question is this: Who is forgiven? Love that is poured into the heart by God's Spirit demonstrates that a person has living faith in Jesus. Instead, faith working through love reveals those whom God can save.

Jesus is our salvation. Our redemption is in Christ through God's grace and mercy. In other words, the redemption that was in Him can become ours by faith, and not by works, because no works we do are good enough to redeem us. Only the works that Christ did, which He credits to us by faith,can bring redemption. Ephesians 2:8–9: "For by grace you have been saved through faith, and that not of yourselves; *it is* the gift of God, not of works, lest anyone should boast." Love for Jesus Christ, and what Jesus went through while on earth, makes it possible for people today to have salvation in Christ for eternity, where there will be no sin. Every person must make their own decision to love as Jesus did while on this earth. Our love for Christ, and obedience to His love,

> **Jesus is our salvation. Our redemption is in Christ through God's grace and mercy.**

will cover our sins (see Prov. 10:12 and 1 Peter 4:8). Having our name on the church books will not save us. We need love for Christ in our heart.

WHAT DID JESUS TEACH ABOUT LOVE WHILE ON EARTH?

Jesus spent three years in ministry on this earth. He didn't try to evangelize His chosen people, Israel. He didn't try to evangelize the non-believing Gentiles. By the lakeside and mountainside, He told parables—simple stories that helped people understand His spiritual kingdom. He held no evangelistic meetings. He told the truth about God to all, Jew or Gentile, and He demonstrated what love looks like at close range (Mark 6:1–6).

Jesus lived and taught love, compassion, and the kingdom of heaven while on earth. When we live and follow what Jesus taught, that looks like justice for those who know the Lord.

God's love doesn't give to get. It never quits when the going gets tough—"when the thrill is gone." God's love was most clearly seen at the cross: utter and total self-sacrifice, not for people who deserved it but for people who needed it. God loves those He created despite their—and our—rebellion.

Paul, of Scripture, tells in 2 Timothy 4:3–4: "For the time will come when they will not endure sound doctrine, but according to their own desires, *because* they have itching ears, they will heap up for themselves teachers; and they will turn *their* ears away from the truth, and be turned aside to fables." Do we see this today with all the different names of different denominations on the front of our churches? The entire history of the Christian church—from Pentecost to the second coming of Jesus—is laid out in the book of Revelation. How are people today to know which church follows the Bible and which follow the traditions of man? If you and I want to be ready for Christ's coming and go home to heaven with those who know about love, please study and know the truth. When we see Christ coming in the clouds, it will be too late to make a choice. Now is the time!

It is through faith that we understand and accept the truth of Christ. Are you a Bible person? Very seldom will people rise higher than their ministers. When the preacher preaches the Word of God, there will be some fruitage for his preaching even though he himself may be a castaway. The ministry is a calling, not a mere profession.

What we see today is seen all through the Bible; it is the reality of free will. God made humans free—He had to, otherwise, we could never truly love Him, and freedom involves the option to do wrong. God also allows us to face the fruit of our wrong decisions: pain, suffering, fear, turmoil, and so forth, all in order to help us realize just what turning away from Him leads to. Free will is wonderful; we couldn't be human without it. Remember, today people do not honor and keep the law of God to be saved; they keep God's law because they are saved and love our Creator God enough to do as God has asked. John 14:21: "He who has My commandments and keeps them, it is he who loves Me." We hear many say they keep Sunday, the first day of the week, holy because Christ rose from the dead on Sunday, the first day of the week. Jesus told people, while He was on earth, "If you love Me, keep My commandments" (John 14:15). We all have to make our choice, just as Lucifer did.

Make your choice today; we are not promised tomorrow. Many will be like the people in Noah's day; they wanted to choose later, but then they didn't have a choice when the rain began to fall.

IS THERE A COUNTERFEIT GOD?

What is God really like? Is He a God of love? Or a God of stern judgment and destruction? Did He make a law He knew nobody could keep?

Don't let anyone tell you there is no pleasure in sin. The Bible says there is and everybody who has indulged in it knows that there is, but it does not last long—it is temporal (see James 4:1–3)..

For every truth God has ever shared with His human children He created, the enemy has created a counterfeit. Sin is deadly; God warned us to stay away from it—it will kill you. "Not so," said Satan. "You will not die; your soul lives on (Gen. 3:4, paraphrase). You're still alive—just in another dimension." How many today, like Eve, believe Satan's lie? We need only to read Genesis 2:7: "God … breathed into his nostrils the breath of life; and man became a living being." Psalm 78:50: "He did not spare their soul from death." Ezekiel 18:4: "The soul who sins shall die." We do not hear this today from those who should know, teachers of God's Word.

So, every truth God has ever shared with us, Satan has a lie that has become the accepted teaching of the majority of even Christians on earth today. When you or I ask a teacher or preacher of the gospel for the truth in God's Bible and they lack evidence for their teachings from the Word of God, trust can be quickly destroyed. This is why God has preserved His Holy Word, that all may know the truth about the love of God for mankind.

Faith is a gift of God, a fruit of the Holy Spirit. We may ask why everyone doesn't have this gift. To receive this gift, we are not to question God's ways or change what He has given in His Holy Word.

In this gift, God gives us freedom and power of choice, and everyone has the freedom and power to accept or reject. Unfortunately, most of the world today choose as the people before the flood. God is love! Think about Jesus and why He chose love to be supreme in everything He created. You and I cannot command or force freedom, friendship, love, or trust. We all know from experience that none of these things can be commanded. We may ask then, "Why did God make a law?" God's law of Ten Commandments is only a law of love—nothing more!

The Good News Bible says that the law was added in order to show what wrong doing is. The Revised English Bible explains that it was "added to make wrong doing a legal offense" (Gal. 3:19). Jesus calls the rules or commandments, the royal law of liberty. "[L]ove *is* the fulfillment of the law" (Rom. 13:10). Paul wants people to know what it means to love (1 Cor. 13:4–6). See also Matthew 22:36–40, Deuteronomy 6:5, and Leviticus 19:18 to learn more about what love is like and what it does.

How do you understand the idea of fearing God? What does it mean, especially in light of the command for us to love God as well? True fear of God is holy; it means that you recognize Him as the ultimate power in the universe. Such fear overcomes any other fear. If God is for you, nobody else can touch you without His permission. If God is against you because you have rebelled against Him, you can run, but you can't hide.

1 John 4:18: "There is no fear in love; but perfect love casts out fear, because fear involves torment. But he who fears has not been made perfect in love." Matthew 10:28: "And do not fear those who kill the body but cannot kill the soul. But rather fear Him who is able to destroy both soul and body in hell."

WHO WILL BE ONE TO SHARE THE TRUTH OF GOD?

The Holy Scriptures give four names to Christians, taken from the four cardinal graces so essential to man's salvation. Notice what they are: They are called saints for their holiness, deliverers for their faith, brethren for their love, and disciples for their knowledge (1 Cor. 1:2, NIV; Heb. 13:1). But how may we have any of these unless we feed upon the Word of God?

The mission of God's true followers is to share the truth of God in His Book with others. Just as Noah appealed to and warned the world to know what was to come upon the world, each Christian should today share the task and privilege to warn the world that Jesus is almost here. And we have to make a decision; no one can do that for us.

The Bible is clear that salvation comes not through church membership but by faith and trust in Christ alone. Anything that is not in harmony with the Word of God cannot and should not be accepted; God is not the author of a law that He knows is impossible to keep. The "law of God" is a law about how people are to love. Anything that is not in harmony with the Word of God cannot be accepted. Love is the most powerful force in the universe and when it becomes the driving source of the power for God's final true followers, the entire world will be confronted with the last eternal decision: loyalty to God and His truth or loyalty to the enemy (primarily in the form of serving self, doing what we think is better).

God needs you to be His voice, His hands, His presence to those blinded by Satan's lies about God's love. God needs you to let Him love people through you. He needs you to let Him live in you so others can see His character of love "close up and personal." If you are in love with Jesus Christ, you will do anything for Him. When we are in love with Jesus Christ, we also aren't timid or self-conscious in the least about telling others about Him. If God knocks on the door of your heart, will you invite Him in?

Sin is sin; it doesn't matter who the victim is. If Jesus had not taken our place in death, that's the penalty we would be staring at. No one will get off by blaming someone else for their sins and Christ's death, when all of us had a part—for everyone has sinned (Rom. 3:23)! It was the sins of all of us that necessitated Christ's sacrifice, that we could have the opportunity to choose a life with our Creator God.

> **God needs you to be His voice, His hands, His presence to those blinded by Satan's lies about God's love.**

Every person needs to ask God to lead them into truth—God does not force His love and truth on anyone. We need to ask for truth because God leaves us with the choice.

OH! THE LOVE OF GOD THE FATHER AND JESUS CHRIST, HIS SON!

In the Bible, we face an issue that should affect us all on the deepest level. In Jesus Christ, we have something unheard of in all history of man and religion: the very Creator God comes to earth as a human being. Jesus relinquishes the privileges and power He had in His past self-existence, puts His life and His entire future existence into the hands of the Father, is born into a family within an occupied nation to live a life that totally reveals God, and then dies for us.

Have you thought of why there was a veil between the Holy and Most Holy Place in the tabernacle, which God had Israel build and carry with them on the way to the Promised Land? This was an active part of worship for the people while Jesus was on earth still. The Most Holy Place represented God's presence, and only the High Priest was allowed to enter once a year to make atonement for the sins of himself and the people. There was a curtain dividing the Holy Place from the Most Holy Place. This curtain was sixty feet high and thirty feet wide and six inches thick. Why did this curtain mean so much then? The presence of God was to be in the Most Holy Place to meet with the High Priest once a year. When Jesus Christ was on the cross, this curtain was torn from top to bottom by the Almighty. This torn curtain was a sign that no longer did man need a priest to take our sins before our Father in heaven. Hebrews 10:19–22 explains that a new High Priest, "Jesus Christ," through the sacrifice of Himself, superseded this ritual for all time and opened for us, through His flesh, access to the throne of our merciful, loving Creator God.

There is no such thing as "many roads that lead to God." Jesus declared: "I am the way, the truth, and the life. No one comes to the Father except through Me" (John 14:6).

"And everyone that has this hope in Him purifies himself, just as He is pure (1 John 3:3). By never once transgressing God's law, "He condemned sin in the flesh" (Rom. 8:3).

The story of Jesus Christ is a love letter—the love of the Father who gave His Son and the love of the Son who gave His life so that all who are willing may ultimately share eternal life in the family of God. Jesus' sacrifice is the final witness, the ultimate statement, of the love God the Father and Jesus Christ had for mankind. 1 John 4:8: "He who does not love does not know God, for God is love." When you and I come to know, as the disciples did, the real Jesus and the real story, it makes all the difference in the world. John 3:17: "For God did not send His Son into the world to condemn the world, but that the world through Him might be saved."

Love is something that cannot be explained; we simply have to experience it firsthand. God's plan provides a way for our sins to be forgiven but is also designed so we would not choose the way of sin again. Mistakenly assuming that Jesus paid the penalty for our sins so we can now do whatever we want, many have a mental picture of Jesus as a quiet, docile, loving being handing out eternal life to anyone who will simply acknowledge Him as Lord and Savior. Many believe there are many roads to heaven and a joyful afterlife. Many have the idea that Jesus died for us to eliminate any requirement that we should obey God—and that a gentle, docile Jesus will admit us into His eternal presence, if we will only acknowledge Him as our Savior, regardless of any way we would choose to live. But to believe these things is to believe in a false Jesus and to completely miss the point of His promised second coming.

Is Christianity a matter of only what Jesus has done for us? Or are we willing to follow Jesus by doing what He commanded and following His example? Jesus explained the laws of the kingdom of God in His sermon on the mount (Matt. 5–7). These are magnifications of the same laws He gave at Sinai, laws that He lived perfectly throughout His entire life on earth. And Jesus said that if a person diminishes them in the least way, that person himself will be regarded as least (Matt. 5:19).

Christianity today has focused on the appealing idea of One who loves you, forgives you, comforts you, and accepts you. But few have explained that Jesus requires His followers to obey the Father's commandments, both for their own good and for the benefit and blessing of all those around them (1 John 2:3–6; 5:3). If you don't understand God's commandments, you don't understand what "sin" is, because sin is the breaking of God's law (1 John 3:4). If you don't understand what sin is, then how can you repent?

Jesus didn't die so we can feel better about ourselves. Jesus died to pay the penalty for the sins you and I have committed. If we return to the life of sin after knowing these things, we crucify again "the Son of God, and put *Him* to an open shame" (Heb. 6:6).

In Luke 6:46 (NIV), Jesus asks a question we should all seriously consider: "Why do you call me, 'Lord, Lord,' and do not do what I say?" Matthew 7:21: "Not everyone who says to Me, 'Lord, Lord,' shall enter the kingdom of heaven, but he who does the will of My Father in heaven." Entering God's kingdom requires living according to God's will. Nothing else will do.

What the world sees as bondage is actually true freedom and happiness in Christ. But that path isn't easy to find, and you alone can make the choice to follow it. "Enter by the narrow gate; for wide *is* the gate and broad *is* the way that leads to destruction, and there are many who go in by it. Because narrow *is* the gate and difficult *is* the way which leads to life, and there are few who find it" (Matt. 7:13–14).

Love is based on trust. It's hard to love another person—friend, spouse, or child—if you don't trust them. A relationship with God works the same way. Through reading the Bible, you will come to know that God is not only trustworthy, He is also the epitome of true love—selfless love—a love that never ceases to forgive. God's goal is not only to forgive us but change us. "If we confess our sins, He is faithful and just to forgive us *our* sins and to cleanse us from all unrighteousness" (1 John 1:9).

God is love and all His actions are based on the motive of selfless love. The life of Jesus demonstrated the character of God. Everything

Jesus did while on this earth was love in action. The same life of love can be yours if you choose to surrender your heart to God. He has promised to live through you. "[F]or it is God who works in you both to will and to do for *His* good pleasure" (Phil. 2:13).

Can you and I imagine how Jesus will feel when He comes? When people will be running away trying to hide, crying for the mountains and rocks to fall on them and hide them from Jesus Christ (Rev. 6:16). Can you imagine how Jesus will feel after He has suffered and died for every person's sins, how much He suffered for each person and the ridicule He suffered from His own people? The matchless love of God for the world that did not love Him, will one day have their choice fulfilled. It is no arbitrary decree on the part of God that excludes the wicked from heaven; they are shut out by their own choice.

Which group do you plan to be part of? Those who will look up and say, "This is my God, I have waited for Him and am ready to go home to heaven with Him"? (Isa. 25:9). Or part of the group that runs and tries to hide from their Creator who loved them enough to come and suffer and die for them?

Don't wait to make your decision later. We are not promised tomorrow. God is waiting for your decision. If you haven't made one yet, consider the results of not making a decision. Many people waited after Noah tried to help the people to believe and come and be saved on the ark. Our God will not make the decision for anyone. Only we can make a choice because God is "love" and love does not force anyone into a decision.

The things that God desires most are lasting peace, freedom, and friendship with His created children. God does not use force for His relationships. If all God wanted was a submission service, He could really have had that in a moment. That is why God gave everything in LOVE and freedom.

Why didn't God destroy Judas after Judas betrayed Jesus to those who crucified Him? Jesus had knelt down and washed the feet of Judas; then Judas went out and betrayed Jesus soon after He had knelt down and washed his feet. Judas would not believe the truth that Jesus was the Son of God and that Jesus came to die for the sins of all mankind, even all the way back to Adam and Eve. Soon after Jesus had washed the feet of Judas, Judas went out and hanged himself (Matt. 27:5). Sin today, as well as then, will self-destruct the person who refuses to believe the truth. All the people who have had the truth known to them and choose not to follow it, will reap the consequence of their choice.

Isaiah 53:4–12 foretells how Jesus would come and die for the sins of all. The choice is left to every person, if he or she will accept the sacrifice that Jesus made that covers all sins. John 3:16, the most well-known verse in the Bible, tells about the love of God for each person on earth. "For God so loved the world that He gave His only begotten Son, that whoever believes in Him should not perish but have everlasting life." Verse 17: "For God did not send His Son into the world to condemn the world, but that the world through Him might be saved." We can read the Scriptures from beginning to end and the resounding theme is that God is a God of love and does not use force.

Remember, Jesus Christ gave Himself and came to us in this world and died for our sins that we could have a life without sin with our Creator God, where there will be no sin, no temptation to sin, because Jesus will destroy sin of all degrees. In place of sin, everyone will be filled with love for our Creator God and for our fellow man. No sin will ever again tempt any person! Sin will be destroyed, including the father of sin and all the angels that followed Lucifer when he was put out of heaven. All those who refused the love of God and refused to love Jesus who came to this earth and suffered and died for

> *Jesus came to die for the sins of all mankind, even all the way back to Adam and Eve.*

every person, will be destroyed, as well as Satan and the angels that chose to follow Satan when he was put out of heaven. The kingdom of God will be a kingdom of love for Jesus Christ, and it will be filled with love for our fellow man.

Have you decided if you will be part of the family that loves God and will live according to His law of love? Every commandment in the law of God is a description of how we need to live and love. There is no force in love; Christ will not decide for any person ever created. We—like Adam and Eve—have to decide for ourself. Only you and

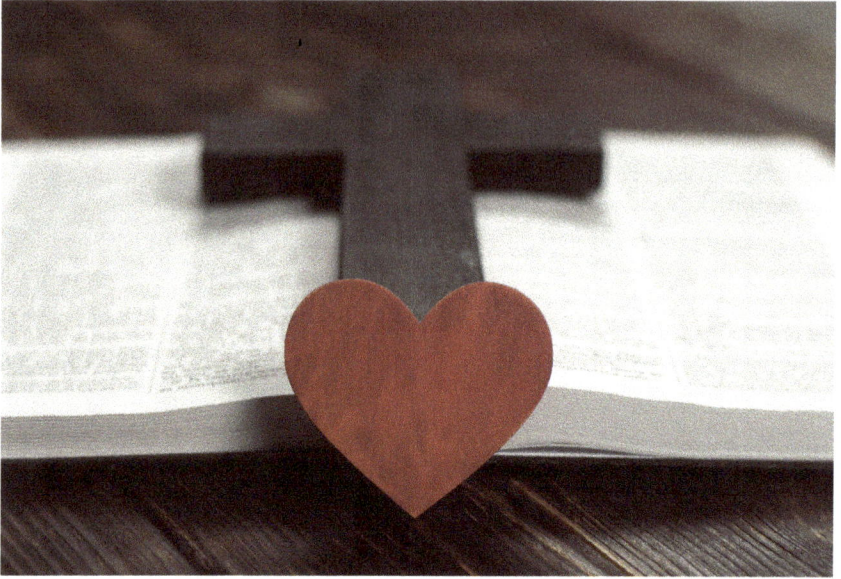

I can decide our future. Will it be eternal life with those who love enough to honor our Creator and fellow man? Or will we choose to be destroyed with Satan and his angels and those who want to believe Satan's lies about the law of God which Satan would not honor and love? You and I cannot force people to be Christians. Jesus Christ never tried to force people to be a Christian or to love Him. Christ loves His creation too much to force them to do for their own good. God is love and the source of love for all His creation. Love cannot be programmed; if it could be, then it's not love!

Jesus Christ will not choose for anyone; we have to choose for ourselves. Love does not use force! Those who will not choose to love God and their fellow man, will one day, before their eternal death, worship God (Rev. 13:8). When Jesus comes, it will be too late then to decide because the judgment will be finished and over before Jesus Christ leaves heaven and comes to earth.

Remember that Jesus Christ came and suffered for your and my sins; He has done all possible that could be done for you and me. The choice is ours, and His love is eternal. There is nothing and no one that can separate you and me from the love of Jesus Christ (Rom. 8:38–39). Make your choice today; we are not promised another day.

Remember, Christ has done all He can do, and He is coming soon to take those with Him who love Him enough to accept His law of love.

There will not be the many different groups that we have on this earth today, but all will be of one accord in their worship. We are told in Isaiah 66:23: "And it shall come to pass *that* from one New Moon to another, and from one Sabbath to another, all flesh shall come to worship before Me," says the LORD." There won't be different groups worshiping on different days; all will be worshiping on the same day. Won't that be a wonderful experience? When all can be of one accord and worship together.

Friend, what is your choice? Jesus Christ came to this earth and suffered shame and ridicule by the people who professed to be His chosen people. These chosen people were to reveal His love to the world but chose to follow those who wanted to worship as they chose and deny the only One who could save them from their sins. Don't do as Cain did in his worship (Gen. 4:3, 5–15). God has made very clear the way and day that He wants those who love Him to worship Him. Christ is worthy because we are created by Him. God is not the kind of person His enemies have made Him out to be—arbitrary, unforgiving, and severe. God is just as loving and trustworthy as His Son, just as willing to forgive and heal. God values nothing higher than the freedom, dignity, and individuality of His intelligent creatures, that their love, their faith, their willingness to listen and obey, may be freely given. He even prefers to regard us not as servants but as friends (John 15:13–15). This is the truth revealed through all the books of Scripture. Don't wait till tomorrow to make your choice; we are not promised another day, week, or year!

God bless you in your choice to be with those who love and are loved by our Creator God!

TEACH Services, Inc.
P U B L I S H I N G

We invite you to view the complete
selection of titles we publish at:
www.TEACHServices.com

We encourage you to write us
with your thoughts about this,
or any other book we publish at:
info@TEACHServices.com

TEACH Services' titles may be purchased in
bulk quantities for educational, fund-raising,
business, or promotional use.
bulksales@TEACHServices.com

Finally, if you are interested in seeing
your own book in print, please contact us at:
publishing@TEACHServices.com
We are happy to review your manuscript at no charge.